KNOWING GOD

A Journey From Information To Intimacy

BRENDALEE BONNIE

KNOWING GOD. Copyright @ 2025. Brendalee Bonnie. All rights reserved.

No part of this publication may be reproduced, stored in a retrieval system or transmitted in any form or by any means, electronic, mechanical, photocopying, recording or otherwise without the prior written permission of the author.

Published by:

Editor: Cleveland O. McLeish (Author C. Orville McLeish)

ISBN: 978-1-965635-85-8 (paperback)

Scripture quotations marked "NKJV" are taken from the New King James Version. Copyright © 1982 by Thomas Nelson, Inc. Used by permission. All rights reserved. Bible text from the New King James Version® is not to be reproduced in copies or otherwise by any means except as permitted in writing by Thomas Nelson, Inc., Attn: Bible Rights and Permissions, P.O. Box 141000, Nashville, TN 37214-1000.

Scripture quotations taken from the Amplified® Bible (AMP). Copyright © 2015 by The Lockman Foundation. Used by permission. www.Lockman.org.

TABLE OF CONTENTS

Introduction	5
Chapter 1: Who is God?	7
Chapter 2: Why Should I Know God?	19
Chapter 3: How to Get to Know God?	35
My Notes	57
The Journey to Destiny Series	59
Aspiring to Inspire	61

INTRODUCTION

Understanding the necessity of knowing God will help us understand our purpose in existence and how we can live a life that pleases and gives glory and honor to Him.

Many may have heard of Him and even met Him, but still do not really know Him.

Knowing God is communing with Him, through Jesus the Son, and having sweet fellowship with the Holy Spirit, our Helper. This is called a relationship. Knowing God is having the lines of communication opened so you can get to know Him better each day and in every way.

Knowing God will help you understand Him in the ways He chooses to speak to you.

Knowing God will help you understand His different qualities and functions.

Knowing God is growing in God. It is being fully engrafted, cultivated, and nurtured in His Word until His Word is who you become, so that you too can become like the Word as you dwell in the earth.

According to Deuteronomy 6:4-5, there is only one true and living God, and we are commanded to love Him wholeheartedly by fearing, obeying, trusting, and honoring Him.

Brendalee Bonnie

*"Hear, O Israel: The L*ORD *our God, the L*ORD *is one! You shall love the L*ORD *your God with all your heart, with all your soul, and with all your strength."*
Deuteronomy 6:4-5 – NKJV

CHAPTER 1

WHO IS GOD?

God is a person, even though He is a spirit. He is *Him* and not *it*. He is the person of the Father and the first in the order of the Godhead or spiritual hierarchy.

Let's see, biblically speaking, the following for further clarity:

In the beginning was the Word, and the Word was with God, and the Word was God. He was in the beginning with God. All things were made through Him, and without Him nothing was made that was made. In Him was life, and the life was the light of men. And the light shines in the darkness, and the darkness did not comprehend it.
John 1:1-5 – NKJV

In the beginning God created the heavens and the earth. The earth was without form, and void; and darkness was on the face of the deep. And the Spirit of God was hovering over the face of the waters.
Genesis 1:1-2 - NKJV

God was from the beginning of time, and He still exists even when time turns into eternity, according to His timing or calendar. This is because of His sovereignty, supremacy, and omnipotence,

God said, *"Let there be,"* and there was. This is seen in the story of creation in Genesis 1-2.

Even to this day, God is still speaking:

Come to Me, all you who labor and are heavy laden, and I will give you rest. Take My yoke upon you and learn from Me, for I am gentle and lowly in heart, and you will find rest for your souls. For My yoke is easy and My burden is light.
Matthew 11:28–30 - NKJV

God is a spirit and the first in the Godhead, or the Trinity. Where His Presence is, there is liberty.

Now the Lord is the Spirit; and where the Spirit of the Lord is, there is liberty.
2 Corinthians 3:17 - NKJV

God, through His Son Jesus and the power of the Holy Spirit, can and will set us free if we believe in Him and allow Him to.

And you shall know the truth, and the truth shall make you free.
John 8:32 - NKJV

Therefore, if the Son makes you free, you shall be free indeed.
John 8:36 - NKJV

To make us free from the curse and judgment which results ultimately in eternal death, God sent His only begotten Son, Jesus Christ, to die for the sins we have committed.

Knowing God

For God so loved the world that He gave His only begotten Son, that whoever believes in Him should not perish but have everlasting life.
John 3:16 - NKJV

For the wages of sin is death, but the gift of God is eternal life in Christ Jesus our Lord.
Romans 6:23 - NKJV

God is Almighty. In Him lies all power, dominion, and authority. He rules and reigns over the entire universe. He is the source of true and real power.

God has spoken once, twice I have heard this: That power belongs to God.
Psalm 62:11 - NKJV

God experiences emotions and, as such, can be touched by the feelings of our infirmities. He is sad and disappointed when we disobey Him. Yes, in this way, we do offend and hurt His feelings. He is happy and pleased when we obey, trust, and serve Him wholeheartedly because for this purpose we were created. Yes, we were indeed created to bring Him glory.

"You are worthy, O Lord, to receive glory and honor and power; For You created all things, and by Your will they exist and were created."
Revelations 4:11 - NKJV

God desires our worship and, not just worship, but true or sincere worship.

God is Spirit, and those who worship Him must worship in spirit and truth."
John 4:24 - NKJV

It takes the spirit man for it to be made possible to really worship God as is required because, in the flesh, no one can ever please God.

Because the carnal mind is enmity against God; for it is not subject to the law of God, nor indeed can be. So then, those who are in the flesh cannot please God. But you are not in the flesh but in the Spirit, if indeed the Spirit of God dwells in you. Now if anyone does not have the Spirit of Christ, he is not His.
Romans 8:7-9 - NKJV

God is essential to your life and the reason for your very existence. He is your Creator and Maker.

So God created man in His own image; in the image of God He created him; male and female He created them.
Genesis 1:27 - NKJV

God is the oxygen or air that we breathe in our lungs. He breathed in us and, as such, breathes through us. Whenever He stops breathing through us, we are no longer living but lifeless beings. This is how supreme He is.

And the LORD God formed man of the dust of the ground, and breathed into his nostrils the breath of life; and man became a living being.
Genesis 2:7 - NKJV

God is the following and more:

1. Loving

He loves not because He is loved. He loves despite not being loved. He looks beyond our faults and flaws and sees our need for salvation and, as such, enables us to experience transformation through the various processes we encounter in life. He loves even when He has been disappointed.

Greater love has no one than this, than to lay down one's life for his friends.
John 15:13 - NKJV

In this the love of God was manifested toward us, that God has sent His only begotten Son into the world, that we might live through Him. In this is love, not that we loved God, but that He loved us and sent His Son to be the propitiation for our sins.
1 John 4:9-10 - NKJV

2. Merciful, Forgiving, and Kind

He doesn't treat us as we deserve because of His patience. His plan is never to harm or hurt but to help.

Now the LORD descended in the cloud and stood with him there, and proclaimed the name of the LORD. And the LORD passed before him and proclaimed, "The LORD, the LORD God, merciful and gracious, longsuffering, and abounding in goodness and truth, keeping mercy for thousands, forgiving iniquity and transgression and sin, by no means clearing the guilty, visiting the iniquity of the fathers upon the children and the children's children to the third and the fourth generation."
Exodus 34:5-7 - NKJV

The Lord is not slack concerning His promise, as some count slackness, but is longsuffering toward us, not willing that any should perish but that all should come to repentance.
2 Peter 3:9 - NKJV

*"For the mountains shall depart and the hills be removed,
But My kindness shall not depart from you,
Nor shall My covenant of peace be removed," Says the L*ORD*, who has mercy on you.*
Isaiah 54:10 - NKJV

*Through the L*ORD*'s mercies we are not consumed, because His compassions fail not. They are new every morning; Great is Your faithfulness.*
Lamentations 3:22-23 - NKJV

Who is a God like You, pardoning iniquity and passing over the transgression of the remnant of His heritage? He does not retain His anger forever, because He delights in mercy. He will again have compassion on us, and will subdue our iniquities. You will cast all our sins into the depths of the sea. You will give truth to Jacob and mercy to Abraham, which You have sworn to our fathers from days of old.
Micah 7:18-20 - NKJV

3. Faithful and True

He doesn't allow you to walk the journey alone or helplessly. He gives us strategies to overcome and cope.

For the LORD God is a sun and shield; The LORD will give grace and glory; No good thing will He withhold from those who walk uprightly.
Psalm 84:11 - NKJV

No temptation has overtaken you except such as is common to man; but God is faithful, who will not allow you to be tempted beyond what you are able, but with the temptation will also make the way of escape, that you may be able to bear it.
1 Corinthians 10:13 - NKJV

"God is not a man, that He should lie, nor a son of man, that He should repent. Has He said, and will He not do? Or has He spoken, and will He not make it good?
Numbers 23:19 - NKJV

4. Perfect and Pure

He is good and perfect, and as such, no impurity is found in Him. Because He is perfect, He was able to look at His handiwork in creation and said that it was good.

Every good gift and every perfect gift is from above, and comes down from the Father of lights, with whom there is no variation or shadow of turning.
James 1:17 - NKJV

As for God, His way is perfect; The word of the LORD is proven; He is a shield to all who trust in Him.
Psalm 18:30 – NKJV

5. Righteous and Just

God has proven Himself to be a righteous and holy God. All this is confirmed in Revelation 4, where the four living creatures and the twenty-four elders paid respect to Him, as before the throne they ascribed unto Him glory, honor, dominion, and power eternally. However, we see the justice of God exhibited through Jesus when He went through the temple, rebuking angrily those who made a mockery of it by misusing it for purposes other than what it was ordained for (see Matthew 21:12-13).

Then Jesus went into the temple of God and drove out all those who bought and sold in the temple, and overturned the tables of the money changers and the seats of those who sold doves. And He said to them, "It is written, 'My house shall be called a house of prayer,' but you have made it a 'den of thieves.'"
Matthew 21:12-13 - NKJV

For the word of God is living and powerful, and sharper than any two-edged sword, piercing even to the division of soul and spirit, and of joints and marrow, and is a discerner of the thoughts and intents of the heart.
Hebrews 4:12 - NKJV

Let the heavens declare His righteousness, for God Himself is Judge. Selah.
Psalm 50:6 - NKJV

Righteousness and justice are the foundation of Your throne; Mercy and truth go before Your face.
Psalm 89:14 - NKJV

Now do not be stiff-necked, as your fathers were, but yield yourselves to the LORD; and enter His sanctuary, which He has sanctified forever, and serve the LORD your God, that the fierceness of His wrath may turn away from you. For if you return to the LORD, your brethren and your children will be treated with compassion by those who lead them captive, so that they may come back to this land; for the LORD your God is gracious and merciful, and will not turn His face from you if you return to Him.
2 Chronicles 30:8-9 - NKJV

but as He who called you is holy, you also be holy in all your conduct, because it is written, "Be holy, for I am holy."
1 Peter 1:15-16 - NKJV

God is balanced in all His ways of thinking, acting, reacting, or responding to the hearts of men towards Him, as seen in Deuteronomy 4:24-31:

For the LORD your God is a consuming fire, a jealous God. "When you beget children and grandchildren and have grown old in the land, and act corruptly and make a carved image in the form of anything, and do evil in the sight of the LORD your God to provoke Him to anger, I call heaven and earth to witness against you this day, that you will soon utterly perish from the land which you cross over the Jordan to possess; you will not prolong your days in it, but will be utterly destroyed. And the LORD will scatter you among the peoples, and you will be left few in number among the nations where the LORD will drive you. And there you will serve gods, the work of men's hands, wood and stone, which neither see nor hear nor eat nor smell. But from there you will seek the LORD your God, and you will find Him if you seek Him with all

your heart and with all your soul. When you are in distress, and all these things come upon you in the latter days, when you turn to the LORD your God and obey His voice (for the LORD your God is a merciful God), He will not forsake you nor destroy you, nor forget the covenant of your fathers which He swore to them.
Deuteronomy 4:24-31 - NKJV

For we must all appear before the judgment seat of Christ, that each one may receive the things done in the body, according to what he has done, whether good or bad.
2 Corinthians 5:10 - NKJV

We begin to know God the Father when we begin to know—not get acquainted with or know about but—know His Son, Jesus Christ, and begin to fellowship with the Holy Spirit, the Helper.

Jesus is the Son of the Father who came to earth in human form to identify with mankind and save them from their sin. Jesus represents His Father God. John 14:6 states that Jesus said He is the Way, the Truth, and the Life, and that no man comes to or is able to approach God the Father unless they come through Him, or, in other words, know Him personally by having a personal relationship with Him. He, Jesus, is the only access to God. Should you try to bypass Jesus, you just missed getting to God.

Jesus said to him, "I am the way, the truth, and the life. No one comes to the Father except through Me. If you had known Me, you would have known My Father also; and from now on you know Him and have seen Him."
John 14:6-7 - NKJV

Knowing God

Knowing God is getting to know the characteristics of Jesus Christ and being like Him by walking in the Spirit, as seen in Galatians 5:16–17 and Galatians 22-23.

Since Jesus is the fullness of the Godhead, then all is in Him. As such, Jesus is exactly what and who God His Father is. Jesus is the Word, so is God. Jesus is Light, so is God. Jesus is Life, so is God. Jesus is the Good Shepherd, so is God. Jesus is the Living Water, so is God. Jesus is the Bread of Life, so is God. Jesus is the Healer, so is God. Jesus is the Deliverer, so is God. We could go on and on. As such, knowing God is knowing Jesus, because no one gains access to the Father unless they go through the Son. All this is summed up in John 1:1-13 and John 14:6.

CHAPTER 2

WHY SHOULD I KNOW GOD?

Firstly, and most importantly, it is necessary to seek to know God because the Word of God tells us that perilous times are coming, and the hearts of men will be deceived with ease if they have no experiential knowledge of God through His Word and personal encounters. Our destiny as it relates to eternity depends solely on this. See the passages of reference below:

But know this, that in the last days perilous times will come: For men will be lovers of themselves, lovers of money, boasters, proud, blasphemers, disobedient to parents, unthankful, unholy, unloving, unforgiving, slanderers, without self-control, brutal, despisers of good, traitors, headstrong, haughty, lovers of pleasure rather than lovers of God, having a form of godliness but denying its power. And from such people turn away! For of this sort are those who creep into households and make captives of gullible women loaded down with sins, led away by various lusts, always learning and never able to come to the knowledge of the truth. Now as Jannes and Jambres resisted Moses, so do these also resist the truth: men of corrupt minds, disapproved concerning the faith; but they will progress no further, for their folly will be manifest to all, as theirs also was.
2 Timothy 3:1-9 - NKJV

For false christs and false prophets will rise and show great signs and wonders to deceive, if possible, even the elect.
Matthew 24:24 - NKJV

Knowing God is important to secure our destiny with Jesus Christ in eternity because no one knows the day or the hour of the return of Christ to take the Bride or His Church away.

But of that day and hour no one knows, not even the angels of heaven, but My Father only. But as the days of Noah were, so also will the coming of the Son of Man be. For as in the days before the flood, they were eating and drinking, marrying and giving in marriage, until the day that Noah entered the ark, and did not know until the flood came and took them all away, so also will the coming of the Son of Man be. Then two men will be in the field: one will be taken and the other left. Two women will be grinding at the mill: one will be taken and the other left. Watch therefore, for you do not know what hour your Lord is coming. But know this, that if the master of the house had known what hour the thief would come, he would have watched and not allowed his house to be broken into. Therefore you also be ready, for the Son of Man is coming at an hour you do not expect.
Matthew 24:36-44 - NKJV

Knowing God is being in a state of readiness or preparedness, like Noah and his family, and the five wise virgins.

And God said to Noah, "The end of all flesh has come before Me, for the earth is filled with violence through them; and behold, I will destroy them with the earth. Make yourself an ark of gopherwood; make rooms in the ark, and cover it inside and outside with pitch. And this is how you shall make it: The length of

the ark shall be three hundred cubits, its width fifty cubits, and its height thirty cubits. You shall make a window for the ark, and you shall finish it to a cubit from above; and set the door of the ark in its side. You shall make it with lower, second, and third decks. And behold, I Myself am bringing floodwaters on the earth, to destroy from under heaven all flesh in which is the breath of life; everything that is on the earth shall die. But I will establish My covenant with you; and you shall go into the ark—you, your sons, your wife, and your sons' wives with you. And of every living thing of all flesh you shall bring two of every sort into the ark, to keep them alive with you; they shall be male and female. Of the birds after their kind, of animals after their kind, and of every creeping thing of the earth after its kind, two of every kind will come to you to keep them alive. And you shall take for yourself of all food that is eaten, and you shall gather it to yourself; and it shall be food for you and for them."
Genesis 6:13-21 - NKJV

Then the L*ORD* *said to Noah, "Come into the ark, you and all your household, because I have seen that you are righteous before Me in this generation. You shall take with you seven each of every clean animal, a male and his female; two each of animals that are unclean, a male and his female; also seven each of birds of the air, male and female, to keep the species alive on the face of all the earth. For after seven more days I will cause it to rain on the earth forty days and forty nights, and I will destroy from the face of the earth all living things that I have made." And Noah did according to all that the* L*ORD* *commanded him. Noah was six hundred years old when the floodwaters were on the earth. So Noah, with his sons, his wife, and his sons' wives, went into the ark because of the waters of the flood. Of clean animals, of animals that are unclean, of birds, and of everything that creeps* *on the earth, two by two they went into the ark to Noah, male and female, as God had commanded Noah. And it came to pass after seven days that the waters of the flood were on the earth. In the six hundredth year of Noah's life, in the second month, the seventeenth day of the month, on that day all the fountains of the great deep were broken up, and the windows of heaven were opened. And the rain was on the earth forty days and forty nights. On the very same day Noah and Noah's sons, Shem, Ham, and Japheth, and Noah's wife and the three wives of his sons with them, entered the ark—they and every beast after its kind, all cattle after their kind, every creeping thing that creeps on the earth after its kind, and every bird after its kind, every bird of every sort. And they went into the ark to Noah, two by two, of all flesh in which is the breath of life. So those that entered, male and female of all flesh, went in as God had commanded him; and the LORD shut him in. Now the flood was on the earth forty days. The waters increased and lifted up the ark, and it rose high above the earth. The waters prevailed and greatly increased on the earth, and the ark moved about on the surface of the waters. And the waters prevailed exceedingly on the earth, and all the high hills under the whole heaven were covered. The waters prevailed fifteen cubits upward, and the mountains were covered. And all flesh died that moved on the earth: birds and cattle and beasts and every creeping thing that creeps on the earth, and every man. All in whose nostrils was the breath of the spirit of life, all that was on the dry land, died. So He destroyed all living things which were on the face of the ground: both man and cattle, creeping thing and bird of the air. They were destroyed from the earth. Only Noah and those who were with him in the ark remained alive.*

Genesis 7:1-23 - NKJV

Then the kingdom of heaven shall be likened to ten virgins who took their lamps and went out to meet the bridegroom. Now five of them were wise, and five were foolish. Those who were foolish took their lamps and took no oil with them, but the wise took oil in their vessels with their lamps. But while the bridegroom was delayed, they all slumbered and slept. And at midnight a cry was heard: 'Behold, the bridegroom is coming; go out to meet him!' Then all those virgins arose and trimmed their lamps. And the foolish said to the wise, 'Give us some of your oil, for our lamps are going out.' But the wise answered, saying, 'No, lest there should not be enough for us and you; but go rather to those who sell, and buy for yourselves.' And while they went to buy, the bridegroom came, and those who were ready went in with him to the wedding; and the door was shut. Afterward the other virgins came also, saying, 'Lord, Lord, open to us!' But he answered and said, 'Assuredly, I say to you, I do not know you.' Watch therefore, for you know neither the day nor the hour in which the Son of Man is coming.
Matthew 25:1-13 - NKJV

Secondly, it is amiss of us to have a form of godliness and deny the true power that really exists through God, which comes with the manifestation of miracles, signs, and wonders.

Paul said that he did not come with sweet words based on head knowledge, but with action or manifestation of the Holy Spirit's power.

I was with you in weakness, in fear, and in much trembling. And my speech and my preaching were not with persuasive words of human wisdom, but in demonstration of the Spirit and of

power, that your faith should not be in the wisdom of men but in the power of God.
1 Corinthians 2:3-5 - NKJV

As such, we were commissioned accordingly by God in Mark 16:14-18 (see also Matthew 28:18-20).

Later He appeared to the eleven as they sat at the table; and He rebuked their unbelief and hardness of heart, because they did not believe those who had seen Him after He had risen. And He said to them, "Go into all the world and preach the gospel to every creature. He who believes and is baptized will be saved; but he who does not believe will be condemned. And these signs will follow those who believe: In My name they will cast out demons; they will speak with new tongues; they will take up serpents; and if they drink anything deadly, it will by no means hurt them; they will lay hands on the sick, and they will recover."
Mark 16:14-18 - NKJV

We also see throughout the Book of Acts of the Apostles that they demonstrated the power of God because of their knowledge of Him.

Thirdly, it is good to know God biblically. This is the first step to salvation; however, it is senseless and useless if this is where it all begins and ends. We must seek to know God experientially or personally. It is from salvation to spiritual maturity to productivity. At every level of our Christian walk, the Presence of God is required, and, as such, there is a need for personal knowledge of Him. This is why Moses, knowing that the call on His life would require that He know God personally, pursued passionately the Presence of God through knowledge of His Ways, not just His acts.

Then Moses said to the Lord, "See, You say to me, 'Bring up this people.' But You have not let me know whom You will send with me. Yet You have said, 'I know you by name, and you have also found grace in My sight.' Now therefore, I pray, if I have found grace in Your sight, show me now Your way, that I may know You and that I may find grace in Your sight. And consider that this nation is Your people." And He said, "My Presence will go with you, and I will give you rest." Then he said to Him, "If Your Presence does not go with us, do not bring us up from here. For how then will it be known that Your people and I have found grace in Your sight, except You go with us? So we shall be separate, Your people and I, from all the people who are upon the face of the earth." So the Lord said to Moses, "I will also do this thing that you have spoken; for you have found grace in My sight, and I know you by name." And he said, "Please, show me Your glory." Then He said, "I will make all My goodness pass before you, and I will proclaim the name of the Lord before you. I will be gracious to whom I will be gracious, and I will have compassion on whom I will have compassion." But He said, "You cannot see My face; for no man shall see Me, and live." And the Lord said, "Here is a place by Me, and you shall stand on the rock. So it shall be, while My glory passes by, that I will put you in the cleft of the rock, and will cover you with My hand while I pass by. [Then I will take away My hand, and you shall see My back; but My face shall not be seen."
Exodus 33:12–23 - NKJV

This is why Moses said that if God's Presence was absent, it would make no sense to move from where he was to do what God had commanded him to do: to take the Israelites forward, across, over, and into the land of promise to access, conquer, and possess.

Moses knew and understood the importance, necessity, and power of the Presence of the Almighty God. He knew that without His Presence, there would be no joy and pleasure in serving, and it would have become a burden. There would be no confidence because of the fear of being harmed during the process. He understood that without God's Presence, there would be no covering because it was His Presence in the form of the pillar of cloud by day and the pillar of fire by night that kept the Egyptians from gaining ground, overtaking, and again enslaving and even harming them.

Fourthly and finally, there are rivers of joy and pleasures unlimited in knowing God as seen in Psalm 16:11.

You will show me the path of life; In Your presence is fullness of joy; At Your right hand are pleasures forevermore.
Psalm 16:11 - NKJV

Knowing God assures us of being continually in His Presence. In His Presence, He shows us the paths of life that lead us to cool, still waters of peace that refresh the soul and sweeten the spirit. In this path, you are led to rivers of joy unknown and pleasures untold, as it is the path of righteousness that leads to the intended destination according to God's thoughts and plans towards us.

At times, what we think is real life is no life at all because this pathway lacks the Presence of God. We are so comfortable with the presents or blessings that we are unaware that we are still empty, void, miserable, and frustrated because God's Presence is not with us, and we are traveling on our own.

Knowing God

Knowing God is the right choice and the best path of life to take if we are to be heading in the right direction.

Knowing God brings streams of joy and rivers of pleasure beyond measure, not sorrow. As such, even in sorrow, He becomes our comfort, peace, and hope for a brighter tomorrow. He takes our cares as we cast them at His feet. In Him, as we come broken, we are made completely whole.

Even in affliction, we will find new songs of praise, adoration, and thanksgiving to sing because of our hope, trust, and confidence which we have placed in Him. There is that assurance that He will deliver us from all evil. Yes, the confidence that He will deliver us from every trap and snare of the enemy, and when we call to Him in times of trouble.

I waited patiently for the Lord; And He inclined to me, and heard my cry. He also brought me up out of a horrible pit, out of the miry clay, and set my feet upon a rock, and established my steps. He has put a new song in my mouth—Praise to our God; Many will see it and fear, and will trust in the Lord.
Psalm 40:1-3 - NKJV

When you know God, you are blessed, because in Him you trust, and when you trust, He will never allow you to fail or be ashamed. He will protect His great name.

For the Scripture says, "Whoever believes on Him will not be put to shame."
Romans 10:11 - NKJV

Stay in His Presence, stay in His Hand, because that is where you belong, and that is where you are made strong. At that place in God, you are being sheltered in the cleft of the rock.

And the Lord said, "Here is a place by Me, and you shall stand on the rock. So it shall be, while My glory passes by, that I will put you in the cleft of the rock, and will cover you with My hand while I pass by. Then I will take away My hand, and you shall see My back; but My face shall not be seen."
Exodus 33:21-23 - NKJV

Knowing and trusting God pays off and pays out big time, all the time. When you know, there is no doubt that the next step is to trust what and who you know because of the conviction and persuasion you now have. Nothing or no one can make you think or do otherwise or steal that trust and commitment you have in His unfailing love.

This is what the joy and pleasure of knowing God does. It is what makes your faith steadfastly grounded in Him and causes you to be inseparable from Him. This joy and pleasure you will find, even in your pain, because of your conviction and confidence that all things work together for good because you know God.

Those who know God, love Him, and are called according to purpose, and absolutely nothing is allowed to separate them from His love.

And we know that all things work together for good to those who love God, to those who are the called according to His purpose.
Romans 8:28 - NKJV

Who shall separate us from the love of Christ? Shall tribulation, or distress, or persecution, or famine, or nakedness, or peril, or sword? As it is written: "For Your sake we are killed all day long; We are accounted as sheep for the slaughter." Yet in all these things we are more than conquerors through Him who loved us. For I am persuaded that neither death nor life, nor angels nor principalities nor powers, nor things present nor things to come, nor height nor depth, nor any other created thing, shall be able to separate us from the love of God which is in Christ Jesus our Lord.
Romans 8:35-39 - NKJV

Do you know Him? If not, do you want to know Him?

To know Him, just say yes to Him and begin to trust Him by following Him as He leads in the path of righteousness. Then and there, you will find that joy and pleasure abundantly and eternally in His Presence and at His Right Hand.

Knowing God is the mission of the hopeful and faithful, and of those who aspire to become like Him. It can be the aspiration of everyone, once you have decided to deny self, take up the cross, and follow Him, as seen in Matthew 16:24.

Knowing God is knowing God's will for our lives. The truth is, God's will for our lives is good, perfect, and acceptable. It will never harm but only help us.

God's will for our lives is documented and can be found in His Word, as seen in Joshua 1:8 and Jeremiah 29:11. It is His will that, with our obedience, we prosper and succeed in every area of our lives, not some. As we prosper spiritually, so is our physical prosperity also within His best interest for us. His will is always to bless and not curse. Conditions also apply, as seen in Isaiah 1:19-20.

If you are willing and obedient, you shall eat the best of the land;
But if you refuse and rebel, you shall be devoured by the sword."
For the mouth of the Lord has spoken.
Isaiah 1:19-20 - AMP

As such, knowing God's will helps us stay on the straight and narrow path by walking by faith and not sight, relying on His strength and not our own might.

Knowing God's will guides and enables us to pray effectively and fervently so that our prayers can avail, prevail against the threats of the enemy, be answered positively, and bear the fruits of testimonies of victory. We will not pray faithless prayers when we know God's will and know we are abiding and trusting accordingly; instead, our prayers will be faith-filled. It is when we know His Will that we will do great exploits, according to Daniel 11:32. That is why Moses sought to know God's Way, because in His will are His ways of doing things.

Knowing God's will is a sign of spiritual maturity, and with maturity comes productivity, because when a tree is mature, it produces its fruit in its season (see Psalm 1:1-3; John 15:1-8).

Knowing God's will enables us to make the necessary sacrifices and apply the appropriate principles in every area of our lives to see God's intended purpose for them.

If we do not know the will of God concerning our lives, we will never be beneficiaries, as seen in Hosea 4:6. Where we know it, we should never ignore or reject it, but embrace it and be empowered and made to prosper because this is how God gets His glory.

We can miss out on God's best interest for us [that is to bless us] if we are ignorant, casual, fearful, doubtful, proud, and disobedient.

We must seek to know, believe God's will, and seek to walk in it fully and not partially, as seen in Hebrews 10:7:

Then I said, 'Behold, I have come To do Your will, O God— [To fulfill] what is written of Me in the scroll of the book.'
Hebrews 10:7 - AMP

Remember, we said before that His will is documented in His Word/the Scroll [The Book/Bible].

According to the passage of focus—Romans 12:2—we will be enabled to walk in God's will when minds have been renewed because they have been transformed. At this level of spiritual maturity, our spirit and soul will be able to conform/adjust or come into agreement with His will and way of doing things.

There will be no struggling, staggering, or wavering to do His bidding. We will then think, speak, and act like God. We will be committed to the ideals/functions/operations of His kingdom.

Knowing God's will will lead us to test and prove it to be good, perfect, acceptable, and true as we practice it daily in our lives and see the results unfold right before our very eyes and those of others looking on.

There is no imperfection in God's will, as seen in Psalm 19:7:

The law of the Lord is perfect (flawless), restoring and refreshing the soul; The statutes of the Lord are reliable and trustworthy, making wise the simple.
Psalms 19:7 - AMP

Doing God's will is never easy, but with maturity, the struggle will end, and it will become a bit easier. It takes a great, strong, and uncommon faith and trust in what He says to follow through patiently as you wait to see Him do what He says He will.

This kind of faith—knowing God's will—enabled Abraham to pass what I would have considered the greatest test of all, as seen in Genesis 22. After waiting for 25 years, he was told to give back the promise, but even here Abraham did not waver, doubted or feared because He knew and understood God's will and His way of doing things.

In His will, God always has a way of doing things His way, not ours. Knowing God is knowing His will and understanding that His ways and thoughts are not like ours, as seen in Isaiah 55:8-9. As we receive this revelation, we will come to know Him by becoming like Him.

We can never pray the prayer of faith for anything, as seen in James 5:15-16, and receive from it if we do not know and believe God's will and pray accordingly. Remember that His will is found in His Word. In other words, if you don't believe it, do not pray it, you will not receive it. Also, do not pray amiss, but be specific by praying in accordance with His Word concerning that which you desire.

Knowing God will make communicating with Him effective and meaningful.

CHAPTER 3

HOW TO GET TO KNOW GOD?

To know God, as Abraham did, requires us to trust and obey and walk by faith and not by sight, hearing or emotions. It is those who know their God who will do great exploits, because their knowledge of Him makes them willing and obedient, and as a result, they will eat the good of the land, as seen in Daniel 11:32 and Isaiah 1:19.

It is those who know their God as Abraham did who will be able to stand the tests of time, to the point that, when challenged, they will walk in obedience and lay their Isaacs down. Knowing God requires trusting His plan completely and placing all in His hands, even when we don't understand.

It was because Abraham knew God that he trusted Him enough to entrust the only son He had promised and given to Him.

It was a knowledge of God that motivated Him to move in total obedience, even though it did not naturally make sense.

It was his knowledge of God that led him to tell his servants that they were going yonder to worship and return, even though he had heard God say that the son was the offering of sacrifice. How then could he and the lad return, if the lad would have then been dead, having been offered as a burnt offering to God? This just did not make sense to the natural man, but to a man who knew his God and trusted Him enough, even when faced with the ultimate test, He trusted Him wholeheartedly and moved in obedience, willingly, not delaying even for a minute (see Genesis 22:1-19).

Abraham was being tested; his faith, loyalty, commitment, love, allegiance, faithfulness, and devotion were being tested. It was the test of all tests. As he partnered with God through His knowledge and a relationship with Him, he passed the test.

Knowing God is letting go and trusting Him because you understand that while you are patiently and joyfully waiting, even when the wait seems to be extending, you are assured that He is favourably working all things together behind the scenes for your good and for His glory (see Romans 8:28).

When we know God, we move in obedience without hesitation and rationalization. This is called faith and trust.

Whilst God was testing to see if Abraham could be trusted with what He had promised, He was also testing Abraham to see if he trusted Him enough.

Knowing God reduces and calms the struggle to move in obedience to His demands or commands.

Knowing God begins and ends with total obedience to Him.

When you know God, you will understand that He will always make a way out of the naturally, seemingly impossible situations; there will be triumph, as seen in 2 Corinthians 2:14.

Abraham returned to his servants delightfully not disappointedly. He returned a victor, not a victim. He returned with a testimony, not a story of tragedy—a testimony of the test passed, a token of good in exchange for his obedience, because of his confidence in the covenant-keeping God (see Genesis 22:5, 8, 19).

Knowing God requires obedience and a willingness to act in accordance with His will, even when it makes no sense and you are not in total agreement with what, how, or when.

This sacrificial obedience comes with benefits, just as disobedience comes with consequences, as seen in Isaiah 1:19-20.

Obedience results in eternal life with God, whilst disobedience results in eternal separation from God.

Obedience results in abundant blessings in this life:

- Being blessed wherever you go.
- Your children and their offspring being blessed.
- God's protection, provision, and preservation.
- Spiritual, mental, emotional, and physical prosperity and success.

When you know God, you agree to follow and serve Him wholeheartedly, willingly, and joyfully, despite the challenges that you may encounter along the journey.

Knowing God is about the act of faith, resisting the temptation to be fearful, and choosing to be faith-filled and faithful.

Obedience is expressing faith and trust in God—you obey because you trust, and because you trust, you obey.

When you know God, you love righteousness and hate sin. You are humble and not prideful. You are submissive to His will, and as a result, you will experience positive outcomes in your life.

Knowing God is understanding and embracing the thoughts and plans He has for you, and trusting His grace to see you through.

Those who know God become a point of reference in heaven and a terror and threat to the gates of hell and, to the enemy, his greatest nightmare.

> *Then the Lord said to Satan, "Have you considered My servant Job, that there is none like him on the earth, a blameless and upright man, one who fears God and shuns evil?"*
> *Job 1:8 - NKJV*

To know God, as Moses and David did, we must come away and camp out with Him and be in His Presence daily. Moses headed up to the mountain, David to the backside of the desert. It calls for solitude and silence, away from the noise, the hustle and bustle, and the busyness of our environment and our soul.

It was there that David testified in Psalm 23 that He was led beside still waters, that his soul was restored, that he was led in the paths of righteousness, and that he was empowered against fear, even as he went through the valley of the shadow of death. God's Presence was his security and comfort. He referred to God's rod and staff, which symbolize the shepherd's concern and compassion for His sheep. The rod conveys the concept of authority, power, discipline, and defense of the sheep. Also, a table was presented before him in the very presence of his enemy because he knew God. Goodness and mercy followed him because he knew God.

This all happened because he sought to know God. Had he not known God, he would not have been empowered in faith to face Goliath, bring him down, and maintain himself when pursued by Saul and many other enemies. He would not have been known to be a man after God's own heart. It was because he knew God that He was known of and by God.

Does God know you? Can He trust you as He did David and Moses with His flock, or that which He desires to entrust into your care: that assignment? Like Abraham, can you be trusted with the lad— that object of blessing? Will you put the blessing above or in place of the one who blessed you with it?

Because He is the Word, you must connect with Him by studying, knowing, and applying His Word daily to your life, as stated in the challenge of Joshua 1:8:

> *This Book of the Law shall not depart from your mouth,*
> *but you shall meditate in it day and night, that you may observe to*
> *do according to all that is written in it. For then you will make*
> *your way prosperous, and then you will have good success.*
> *Joshua 1:8 - NKJV*

You must worship Him unconditionally, regardless of what is happening in your life. The songwriter says that when trouble is in your life, that is when you must raise it and give God some crazy praise. Remember the good times in the bad times and use this as a platform to build your altar of sacrificial praise right in the face of the enemy.

I will bless the LORD at all times; His praise shall continually be in my mouth. My soul shall make its boast in the LORD; The humble shall hear of it and be glad. Oh, magnify the LORD with me, and let us exalt His name together. I sought the LORD, and He heard me, and delivered me from all my fears. They looked to Him and were radiant, and their faces were not ashamed. This poor man cried out, and the LORD heard him, and saved him out of all his troubles. The angel of the LORD encamps all around those who fear Him, and delivers them. Oh, taste and see that the LORD is good; Blessed is the man who trusts in Him! Oh, fear the LORD, you His saints! There is no want to those who fear Him. The young lions lack and suffer hunger; But those who seek the LORD shall not lack any good thing.
Psalm 34:1-10 - NKJV

You must live an active and effective prayer life. This is done by cultivating a praying spirit. If we are to always pray without ceasing, this includes talking to God about any and everything, at any time and anywhere. You communicate with Him in your spirit as the thoughts come, whether they be good or evil. As you identify them, communicate or talk to God; accordingly, either silently or audibly, as the Spirit of Truth or the Holy Spirit leads you. When we pray this way, it is guaranteed that we will not faint or fail, because strength is released to sustain us in our times of need.

pray without ceasing,
1 Thessalonians 5:17 - NKJV

*praying always with all prayer and supplication in the
Spirit, being watchful to this end with all perseverance
and supplication for all the saints—
Ephesians 6:18 - NKJV*

You must always have a heart of thanksgiving or an attitude of gratitude. Cultivating a sweet spirit that will attract you to Him and He to you and others to you and, eventually, also to Him.

*Rejoice always, in everything give thanks; for this is the will of
God in Christ Jesus for you.
1 Thessalonians 5:16,18 - NKJV*

*Make a joyful shout to the LORD, all you lands! Serve
the LORD with gladness; Come before His presence with singing.
Know that the LORD, He is God; It is He who has made us, and not
we ourselves; We are His people and the sheep of His
pasture. Enter into His gates with thanksgiving, and into His
courts with praise. Be thankful to Him, and bless His name. For
the LORD is good; His mercy is everlasting, and His
truth endures to all generations.
Psalm 100:1-5 - NKJV*

Everybody ought to know who God is if they are to be enabled to serve Him faithfully and in sincerity. This will help in understanding how He operates and does things. This helps one to truly honor, obey, trust, respect, reverence, and fear Him, and remain committed to Him.

Knowing God is knowing and understanding who He really is. When you begin to know and understand, then you will know what He can do and how it is done. It is not about knowing Him only from what has been said or what He has done, but about who He really is—His ways, thoughts, and approach to doing things. It is getting to know Him through personal experience, through a relationship with Him. This comes from fellowshipping with Him daily and truly allowing Him to be Savior, Lord, and King of your life.

Going on daily dates with Him through scheduling quality, quiet times in His Presence is essential, just like breathing and consuming water. As you consume the physical manna or food to be nurtured and developed and sustained, likewise, you should desire the spiritual manna, which is written in His Word.

Soaking and just basking, worshiping, and reflecting as you wait with Him in silence is highly recommended. Be expectant when you enter and be open to receiving as you wait patiently, not being bombarded with anxious, disturbing thoughts. Where these are found to be present, begin to cast them at His feet as if emptying a boat that is about to sink so that you will stay afloat on the water. In so doing, this is preventing the unwanted from entering in and spoiling those extremely important moments; being shut-in with God. Then you just begin to let your spirit stay afloat and be carried away and led by the Holy Spirit.

One's first and foremost aspiration in life should be to know God for who He really is. Knowing God is seeing Him as your everything and, as such, depending on Him in everything. Knowing God will help one in their perspective on life and perception about life and all that it entails. It will help one who desires to do all, to the best of their ability, according to His commands and precepts, to please Him.

Desiring to know God will cause you to understand and embrace the truth that it is not about you, but all about Him. Without Him, there would have been nothing, not even for us to enjoy. We would not even be in existence. Life is all because of Him, and as such, should be spent with and for Him. This is how we will truly experience true fulfilment in being alive or existing.

When you seek to know God, it will cause you to always seek to have His Word hidden in the heart so that it prevents sinning against, offending, or displeasing Him.

How can a young man cleanse his way? By taking heed according to Your word.
Psalm 119:9 - NKJV

Your word I have hidden in my heart, that I might not sin against You.
Psalm 119:11 - NKJV

Your word is a lamp to my feet and a light to my path.
Psalm 119:105 - NKJV

Let the words of my mouth and the meditation of my heart be acceptable in Your sight, O LORD, my strength and my Redeemer.
Psalm 19:14 - NKJV

When you know God as a believer, He prevents you from falling and will present you faultless before His throne with great pride and joy. He protects you from all evil, so even though weapons are formed against you, they will not prosper. He will preserve your soul so that when the enemy comes in like a flood and seeks to accuse you and sift you, the Holy Spirit lifts a standard against it and, as such, God blocks and stops it. This, my friend, is the benefit of knowing God.

Knowing God makes you, like David, confident in Him, so much so that, even in hard times, you too can declare Him to be your shepherd. You can know Him as your helper, keeper, navigator, protector, defender, shield and buckler, sustainer, provider, and healer. Your confidence will then grow and soar because of your experience, which gives you high expectations of Him.

Knowing God as a sinner in need of a Savior frees you from the curse of sin, which the penalty is death.

For the wages of sin is death, but the gift of God is eternal life in Christ Jesus our Lord.
Romans 6:23 - NKJV

Knowing God as both believer and sinner brings one into true freedom through knowledge and experience of the Truth, as seen in John 8:32 and 36 and John 14:6.

Jesus said to him, "I am the way, the truth, and the life. No one comes to the Father except through Me."
John 14:6 - NKJV

This truth brings conviction of salvation, not condemnation. It also brings freedom.

There is therefore now no condemnation to those who are in Christ Jesus, who do not walk according to the flesh, but according to the Spirit. For the law of the Spirit of life in Christ Jesus has made me free from the law of sin and death. For what the law could not do

in that it was weak through the flesh, God did by sending His own Son in the likeness of sinful flesh, on account of sin: He condemned sin in the flesh.
Romans 8:1-3 – NKJV

And you shall know the truth, and the truth shall make you free."
John 8:32 - NKJV

Therefore if the Son makes you free, you shall be free indeed.
John 8:36 - NKJV

The following are a few of the many persons whose life stories and experiences are recorded in the Word of God; they knew God, and their lives were examples of greatness, excellence, and great exploits:

- Noah
- Abraham
- Moses
- Joshua
- Joseph
- David
- Daniel
- Paul
- Peter

The next step after knowing God is to be like Him, loving as He loves, thinking as He does, and acting and responding to situations and things as He would have. Yes, knowing Him is emulating or imitating Him by becoming who He is.

Not knowing God is living an empty, meaningless, and careless life. It is a life without a sense of purpose; it is pointless and as useless as a pencil without a point or an eraser. It simply doesn't add up in the end and results in a total loss when you have completed the years He has allotted to you, only to see that you end up in regret and at the wrong destination, and not the one God had planned for you.

For I know the thoughts that I think toward you, says the LORD, thoughts of peace and not of evil, to give you a future and a hope.
Jeremiah 29:11 - NKJV

And he showed me a pure river of water of life, clear as crystal, proceeding from the throne of God and of the Lamb. In the middle of its street, and on either side of the river, was the tree of life, which bore twelve fruits, each tree yielding its fruit every month. The leaves of the tree were for the healing of the nations. And there shall be no more curse, but the throne of God and of the Lamb shall be in it, and His servants shall serve Him. They shall see His face, and His name shall be on their foreheads. There shall be no night there: They need no lamp nor light of the sun, for the Lord God gives them light. And they shall reign forever and ever.
Revelation 22:1-5 - NKJV

Knowing God is trusting Him and taking Him at His Word. When you know God, your approach to Him is one of humility and confidence; we see this in Psalm 51 and Psalm 16:1-2.

When you know God, you see your weakness and remember and acknowledge His strength.

And He said to me, "My grace is sufficient for you, for My strength is made perfect in weakness." Therefore most gladly I will rather boast in my infirmities, that the power of Christ may rest upon me.
2 Corinthians 12:9 - NKJV

When you know God, the joy of the Lord becomes your source of strength, and you are then empowered and enabled to do great exploits and become great in Him.

Then he said to them, "Go your way, eat the fat, drink the sweet, and send portions to those for whom nothing is prepared; for this day is holy to our Lord. Do not sorrow, for the joy of the LORD is your strength."
Nehemiah 8:10 - NKJV

Those who do wickedly against the covenant he shall corrupt with flattery; but the people who know their God shall be strong, and carry out great exploits.
Daniel 11:32 - NKJV

I will make you a great nation; I will bless you and make your name great; and you shall be a blessing. I will bless those who bless you, and I will curse him who curses you; And in you all the families of the earth shall be blessed.
Genesis 12:2-3 - NKJV

Knowing God makes you unmovable, unshakeable, and unstoppable.

O Lord, You are the portion of my inheritance and my cup; You maintain my lot. The lines have fallen to me in pleasant places;

Yes, I have a good inheritance. I will bless the Lord who has given me counsel; My heart also instructs me in the night seasons. I have set the Lord always before me; Because He is at my right hand I shall not be moved.
Psalm 16:5-8 - NKJV

Knowing God is making Him Lord [Ruler and Master] of your life.

In knowing God, not even death separates us from Him. Even in death are the paths of life when we are in His Presence and at His right hand. There we will find eternal joy and pleasures unknown and untold, and will live with Him together forever, undisturbed or perturbed by earth's sorrows, stress, woes, trials and pains, heartaches, and persecutions. There and then, all tears will be wiped away from the eyes. As such, when you know God, even in death, we win, because we will rise to receive that eternal prize: eternal life.

Precious in the sight of the LORD Is the death of His saints.
Psalm 116:15 - NKJV

We are confident, yes, well pleased rather to be absent from the body and to be present with the Lord.
2 Corinthians 5:8 - NKJV

For You will not leave my soul in Sheol, nor will You allow Your Holy One to see corruption.
Psalm 16:10 – NKJV

Knowing God

Now thanks be to God who always leads us in triumph in Christ, and through us diffuses the fragrance of His knowledge in every place.
2 Corinthians 2:14 - NKJV

Knowing God is "having the fear of God" upon your life. Fearing God is overlooking man's opinion and valuing God's decision over even yours.

Lack of fearing God will and can attract His anger or wrath to the point of Him punishing us.

Remember what the Hebrew writer said, *"It is a fearful thing to fall into the hands of the living God." (Hebrews 10:31 - NKJV)*. God became angry over the wickedness of the cities of Sodom and Gomorrah. We all know the story, and we all know the result of God's anger.

Let us hear the conclusion of the whole matter: Fear God and keep His commandments, for this is man's all.
Ecclesiastes 12:13 - NKJV

When we fear God, we keep His commandments. The whole duty or responsibility of man is to fear God and keep His commands.

As such, when we fear God, we do not rely solely on the physical bread for our survival and sustenance, but on the Bread of Life, Jesus Christ, who is the Word of Life, the ultimate living sacrifice who gave His life as a ransom for all.

But He answered and said, "It is written, 'Man shall not live by bread alone, but by every word that proceeds from the mouth of God.'"
Matthew 4:4 - NKJV

And Jesus said to them, "I am the bread of life. He who comes to Me shall never hunger, and he who believes in Me shall never thirst."
John 6:35 - NKJV

For God so loved the world that He gave His only begotten Son, that whoever believes in Him should not perish but have everlasting life.
John 3:16 - NKJV

When we fear God, we walk in wisdom, and walking in wisdom is fearing God. In doing so, you gain knowledge and understanding of the true and living God.

"The fear of the Lord is the beginning of wisdom, and the knowledge of the Holy One is understanding.
Proverbs 9:10 - NKJV

As such, knowing and fearing God means doing all the above, which is summed up this way: keep His commands by living in accordance with the standards of His Word, which teaches and helps us, through the help of the Holy Spirit, to fear and honor Him.

When we do, we do not live carnally but spiritually. Yes, we walk in the spirit and not in the flesh.

Now the works of the flesh are evident, which are: adultery, fornication, uncleanness, lewdness, idolatry, sorcery, hatred, contentions, jealousies, outbursts of wrath, selfish ambitions, dissensions, heresies, envy, murders, drunkenness, revelries, and the like; of which I tell you beforehand, just as I also told you in time past, that those who practice such things will not inherit the kingdom of God. But the fruit of the Spirit is love, joy, peace, longsuffering, kindness, goodness, faithfulness, gentleness, self-control. Against such there is no law.
Galatians 5:19-23 - NKJV

The flesh fails, but the spirit never fails because the spirit man is connected to God through Jesus the Son, and Jesus never fails.

If we rely on the Holy Spirit to work through us, with our spirit, we will overcome and conquer the works or lusts of the flesh, which is to sin. All this is made possible when we have Jesus Christ, or the Spirit of God [the Holy Spirit], truly living within us.

Therefore, if anyone is in Christ, he is a new creation; old things have passed away; behold, all things have become new.
2 Corinthians 5:17 - NKJV

Knowing and fearing God is simple yet extremely profound and necessary if we are to please Him, one day meet Him face to face, and live with Him eternally. That is why God sent Jesus, and Jesus came obediently to die for our sins to redeem us permanently and give us residency with Him in heaven or eternity.

Knowing God and fearing God is the only way to truly succeed in life, to prosper in all our ways and in all our being, and to do things.

Trust in the Lord with all your heart, and lean not on your own understanding; In all your ways acknowledge Him, and He shall direct your paths. Do not be wise in your own eyes; Fear the Lord and depart from evil.
Proverbs 3:5-7 - NKJV

Knowing and fearing God should never be taken lightly or approached casually, but should be done intentionally and sincerely.

Jesus said to him, 'You shall love the Lord your God with all your heart, with all your soul, and with all your mind.'
Matthew 22:37 - NKJV

It is loving God unconditionally, whether in good times or bad, happy, or sad. This is all that really makes that significant difference in our lives.

Knowing and fearing God is remembering and honoring Him in the fruit of one's youth, whilst there is yet strength; giving God the best of our days; the first or one tenth of everything and every area therewith. Tithe, sacrifice, and offering our lives to Him is our ultimate sacrifice because it must cost us something to know and follow Him as disciples of Christ.

Remember now your Creator in the days of your youth, before the difficult days come, and the years draw near when you say, "I have no pleasure in them": While the sun and the light, the moon and the stars, are not darkened, and the clouds do not return after the rain; In the day when the keepers of the house tremble, and the strong men bow down; When the grinders cease because they are few, and those that look through the windows grow dim; When

the doors are shut in the streets, and the sound of grinding is low; When one rises up at the sound of a bird, and all the daughters of music are brought low. Also they are afraid of height, and of terrors in the way; When the almond tree blossoms, the grasshopper is a burden, and desire fails. For man goes to his eternal home, and the mourners go about the streets. Remember your Creator before the silver cord is loosed, or the golden bowl is broken, or the pitcher shattered at the fountain, or the wheel broken at the well. Then the dust will return to the earth as it was, and the spirit will return to God who gave it. "Vanity of vanities," says the Preacher, "All is vanity."
Ecclesiastes 12:1-8 - NKJV

I write to you, fathers, because you have known Him who is from the beginning. I write to you, young men, because you have overcome the wicked one. I write to you, little children, because you have known the Father.
1 John 2:13 - NKJV

and that from childhood you have known the Holy Scriptures, which are able to make you wise for salvation through faith which is in Christ Jesus.
2 Timothy 3:15 - NKJV

Remember God, know and begin to fear Him today before it is too late. Despite the stage of life you are currently at, whether it is morning, noon, or night, it is not too late to seek to know and begin to fear God. As His Word says in Hebrews 3:15, today if you hear His voice, harden not your heart. Be not smart or foolish, but wise and press towards the mark of the prize of the higher calling which is in Jesus Christ our Lord, as seen in Philippians 3:13-14.

According to John 9:4, we must work while it is day, because the night will come when working will become impossible.

Knowing and fearing God is not being wise in our own eyes but seeing through His eyes and pressing towards the eternal prize.

Oh, the joys and pleasures of knowing God; it comes loaded with heavenly benefits. The conclusion is, at the end of the day or the year and days of our life, it is knowing and fearing God that matters most, because this is the whole duty or responsibility for the existence of mankind. Everything else will fade and fail, but only God and His Word will stick and stay or last forever, as seen in Isaiah 40:6-8.

The voice said, "Cry out!" And he said, "What shall I cry?" "All flesh is grass, and all its loveliness is like the flower of the field. The grass withers, the flower fades, because the breath of the Lord blows upon it; Surely the people are grass. The grass withers, the flower fades, but the word of our God stands forever."
Isaiah 40:6-8 - NKJV

The whole duty of man is to be responsible and wise by fearing God.

As one worshipper and songwriter penned and sang, *"When you know Him, you will find me."* Knowing God is finding your identity. There is no end to knowing Him; as such, this pursuit is unto eternity. If you desire to know God, then by all means seek Him wholeheartedly, and you will surely find Him, because He hides so that we can search for Him.

Knowing God

And you will seek Me and find Me, when you search for Me with all your heart.
Jeremiah 29:13 - NKJV

God is an amazing, incredible, and infinite being, and yes, He is for real. He exists. He doesn't need anyone to be the God He is. He is God all by Himself.

As such, in conclusion, knowing God is relationship over religion, revelation over emotion, intimacy over unfamiliarity—being practical in applying His principles, precise, fully persuaded, and striving towards spiritual perfection in Christ, as seen in James 1:4 and 1 Peter 13-16. Knowing God requires girding up your loins, guarding your heart with all due diligence, and being vigilant and sober.

MY NOTES

THE JOURNEY TO DESTINY SERIES

Copies are available on Amazon, both in Kindle and paperback

OTHER PURCHASING OPTION:

Email (*for paperback only*): Dailymannadevotionals@gmail.com

ASPIRING TO INSPIRE

My heart is overflowing with a good theme; I recite my composition concerning the King; my tongue is the pen of a ready writer. (Psalm 45:1 – NKJV).

The Lord GOD has given me the tongue of the learned, that I should know how to speak a word in season to him who is weary. He awakens me morning by morning, He awakens my ear to hear as the learned. (Isaiah 50:4 – NKJV).

BLB MY QUOTES

"Being productive in my place of affliction: my pain producing purpose. As a result, you are reading because I was bleeding, and I choose to make my meditation be my medication."

BLB MY QUOTES

"Like an oyster hidden in the pearl of great price for which you have to dig deep in order to seek; so is your purpose hidden in your pain and is revealed at a great price called sacrifice, so that your story can become God's glory."

THE JOURNEY TO DESTINY
SERIES

Knowing God, as divinely inspired by the Holy Spirit, was written by the author, Brendalee Bonnie, of St. Catherine, Jamaica.

This book, as with all the others in the Journey to Destiny Series, was revealed to me during quiet times spent with God in His Presence, where the deep and secret things are revealed, and instructions are given. As I seek His face and wait, He speaks, and I begin to write as I hear.

As I am challenged, strengthened, encouraged, and comforted accordingly, I aspire to inspire others who are seeking answers, strength, and direction on the Journey to Destiny.

Finding and knowing the truth is the only way to be truly made free indeed, and this truth is found in God's Word by which I am inspired to write.

I thank the God of heaven that He has used me to be a ready writer to give a word to those who need it in times of need as they seek. I understand what it is like to be on the receiving end, because when His Spirit speaks to me, He relieves my troubled mind. His voice indeed makes the biggest difference one can ever find. He speaks all the time, but the deep secrets are revealed in the secret place as you set quality quiet time to seek His face and wait as you receive His grace.

The objective of this book is to help the reader understand the importance of knowing God personally, not just by what has been heard, seen, and read. When you know God personally or experientially, His existence and power are unquestionable and undeniable, and will not be a figment of one's imagination, but instead, their reality. Then you will be fully persuaded in your knowledge of what and why you believe, which forms the foundation of your faith in God.

THE JOURNEY TO DESTINY
S E R I E S

Brendalee Bonnie was born in the parish of St. Catherine. She gave her life to the Lord at the tender age of sixteen. Her passion is singing and living for God. Later in her life, with a new mandate and call of God on her life, she realized she has a passion to inspire people, not just on a spiritual level but in every other aspect of life.

Brendalee's passion for God and for helping others motivated her to successfully complete the level one counseling course at WAFIF Christian College (WCC). This accomplishment was ordained by God because it allowed her to get the proper training needed to professionally and effectively develop a God-given gift nestled within her.

As the Bible states in 2 Timothy 3:15-17, it is important to be equipped and thoroughly furnished for every good work. This course also confirmed the assignment as a helper/encourager, thereby confirming the prompting and passion to share in order to heal and empower others by giving strength to the weak, inspiration to the weary, and salvation to the lost.

With the heart of a servant, her tongue has been made the pen of a ready writer, one of the learned. The message of encouragement and empowerment is thereby communicated through her writing, giving a word in season to those who need it.

As commissioned in Luke 4:18-19 and Isaiah 61:1-2, Brendalee has answered the call to help heal the brokenhearted and to help them experience true freedom through her life-changing spiritual encounter, as it is shared in this book. The objective is to help as she has been helped, and to help deliver and liberate, as she has been delivered and liberated, as the truth is revealed. Her desire is to identify with others in their struggles in the areas she has struggled in and help them get out, as she got out through God's help.

In her professional career, Brendalee works as an Administrative Assistant. She thoroughly enjoys her job, the highest point of which involves interacting with people at all levels. Each challenge encourages and pushes her to improve her personality, perception of others, and people skills. Her strengths are being passionate about God and helping, encouraging, comforting, and caring for the needs of others.

www.ingramcontent.com/pod-product-compliance
Lightning Source LLC
Chambersburg PA
CBHW071230160426
43196CB00012B/2472